snowflakes

FOR ALL SEASONS

snowflakes

FOR ALL SEASONS

72
EASY-TO-MAKE
SNOWFLAKE PATTERNS

BY CINDY HIGHAM

Gibbs Smith, Publisher
Salt Lake City

First Edition
08 07 06 05   5 4 3 2

Text and illustrations © 2004 Cindy Higham

Published by
Gibbs Smith, Publisher
P.O. Box 667
Layton, Utah 84041

Orders: 1.800.748.5439
www.gibbs-smith.com

Designed by Dawn DeVries Sokol
Printed and bound in The United States of America

Library of Congress Control Number:

2004108618

contents

getting started

IT'S OFTEN SAID that no two snowflakes are alike. That's also true with paper snowflakes! The slightest change in the paper folding or the slightest cut difference and you can have a new and exciting snowflake.

Use the patterns in this book to learn the techniques, and then start experimenting on your own.

Snowflakes could be the least expensive decoration you can make. Any 8½ x 11 sheet of paper will do. There are many different paper styles and colors available for choosing. Find some paper and a pair of *sharp* scissors and you are ready to start.

Use the diagrams on page 8 to learn how to fold your paper. Then pick the pattern you want to try first.

You can use the same patterns many times. Photocopy or trace the patterns rather than cutting them out so you can use them many times.

You can also photocopy your patterns smaller or larger so you have a variety of snowflake sizes for decorating. Cut a piece of paper to the size you want your snowflake. Fold the paper, as per the instructions, then enlarge or reduce the pattern to fit your snowflake triangle.

Hints

Put a small piece of tape on the sides of your pattern and tape it to your folded paper. Cut the small sections out first and work your way up to the large cuts. This will give you more paper to hold onto for a longer amount of time.

You can tape the finished snowflakes to your windows or hang them from the ceiling with thread. Watch the room transform into a magical place.

If your snowflakes aren't flat, you can press them into a book for a few days or you can take a slightly warm iron and press out the folds.

If you want to make your snowflakes sparkle, you can buy glue sticks with glitter in them or glue glitter pens that are fun to decorate your snowflakes with.

Use colored paper that coordinates with the holiday you are celebrating.

Fun Uses for Snowflakes
Bows for packages
Scrapbook fillers
Picture frames
Bulletin board borders
Window displays
Cards
Valentines
Invitations
Holiday tree decorations
Placemats

Folding Instructions

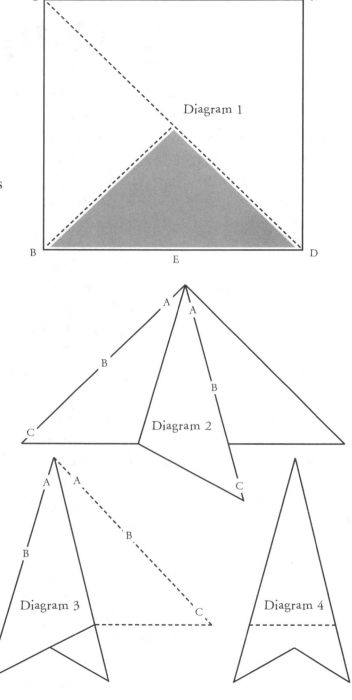

Diagram 1

Fold corner A down to B. (After each fold, run your fingernail along the fold to press it down tight.)

Fold corner C down to D.

If you are using 8 1/2 x 11 paper you will need to cut off the tail along line E. If you use square paper as shown in the diagram, you will not have a tail to cut off. You should have a triangle that looks like the shaded area on the diagram.

Diagram 2

Fold the triangle into equal thirds starting with the left side. Fold A to A, B to B, and C to C.

Diagram 3

Now fold in the opposite third. Fold A to A, B to B, and C to C. The more perfect the paper is folded the more perfect the snowflake will be.

Diagram 4

Your paper should now look like this. On one side of the folded paper you will see a straight line, where the dotted line is shown in the diagram. Cut off the paper along this line. You now have your snowflake triangle and are ready to choose a pattern to make. Choose a pattern to cut out.

New Year's Hour Glass

Hearts with Arrows

12

Burst of Hearts

Cupid

Lincoln and Washington

Shamrocks-a-Plenty

Butterflies

Tulip Garden

23

SPRING

Love Birds

24

Lilies and Baby Chicks

Ring around the Rosies

Sunshine, Clouds, and Lightning

Swinging in a Tree

Firecrackers and Liberty Bells

Freedom Stars

Statue of Liberty

Pumpkins and Autumn Leaves

Autumn Leaves

Black Cats and Jack-o-lanterns

Big Bats

Spiders Everywhere

Owls and Black Cats

42

43

Spiderweb

Turkey Time

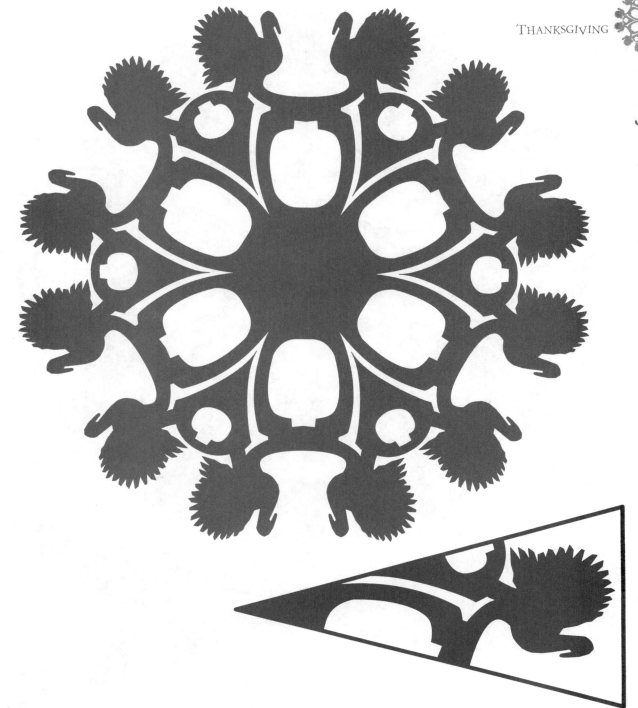

Thanks to the Pilgrims

Toy Soldiers

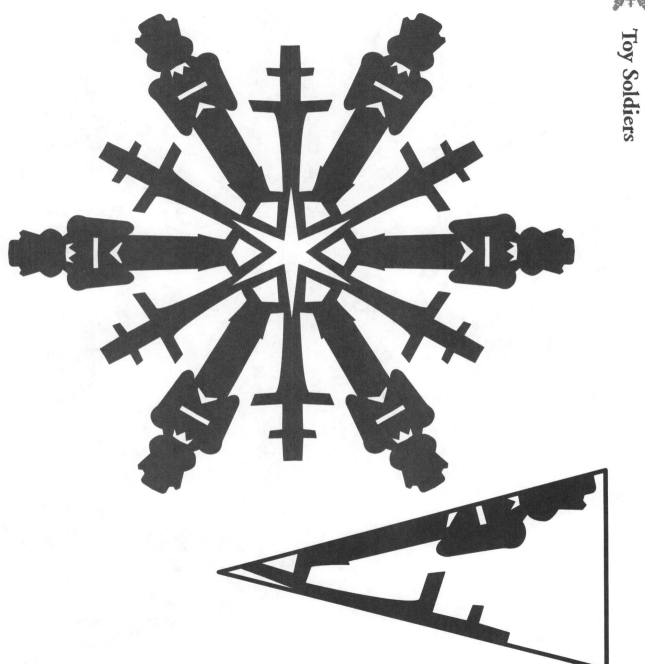

Nutcracker Ballerina

49

Christmas Bells

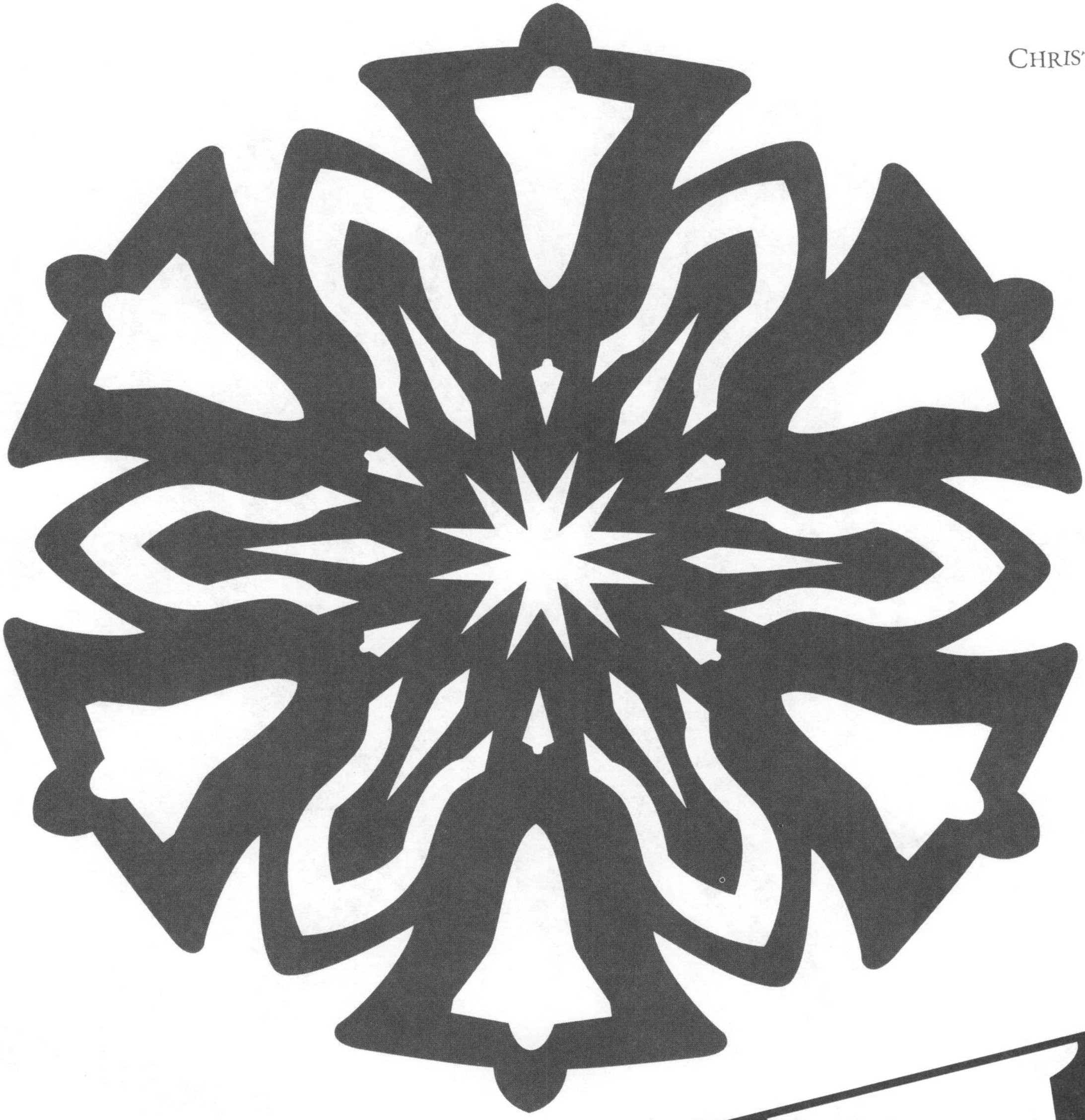

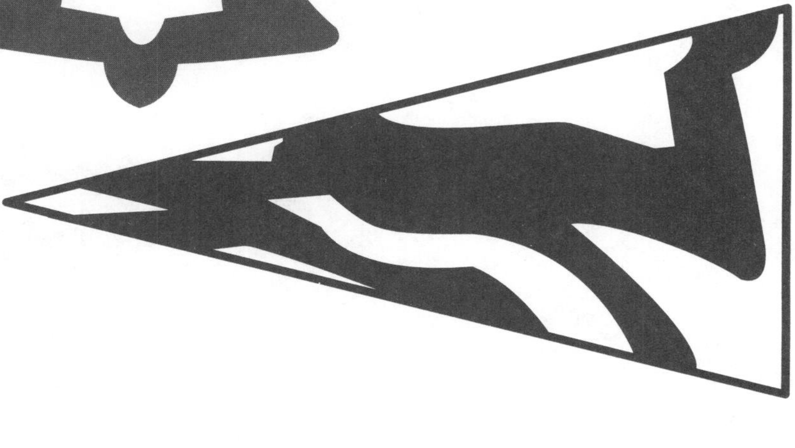

Candlelight

Let's Make a Snowman

53

Powerline

Jack Frost

Pinecone

60

61

Empty Heart

Pinecone Lace

Thistle

Teddy Bears

Have a Ball

Dog

Cat

73

Venus Flytrap

Aliens

Football

Pinwheel